Y0-AFP-165

# LIGHTNING, HURRICANES, and BLIZZARDS

| The Science of STORMS |

Paul Fleisher

LERNER PUBLICATIONS COMPANY · MINNEAPOLIS

Lerner Publications Company
A division of Lerner Publishing Group, Inc.
241 First Avenue North
Minneapolis, MN 55401 U.S.A.

Website address: www.lernerbooks.com


Library of Congress Cataloging-in-Publication Data

Fleisher, Paul.
    Lightning, hurricanes, and blizzards : the science of storms /
by Paul Fleisher.
        p.   cm. — (Weatherwise)
    Includes bibliographical references and index.
    ISBN 978-0-8225-7536-8 (lib. bdg. : alk. paper)
    1. Lightning—Juvenile literature.  2. Hurricanes—Juvenile
literature.  3. Blizzards—Juvenile literature.  I. Title.
QC966.5.F54  2011
551.55—dc22                                          2009044918

Manufactured in the United States of America
1 – PC – 7/15/10

# CONTENTS

**4** INTRODUCTION

**8** CHAPTER ONE
## Air Masses, Weather Fronts, and Midlatitude Cyclones

**15** CHAPTER TWO
## Thunderstorms

**23** CHAPTER THREE
## Tornadoes

**29** CHAPTER FOUR
## Hurricanes

**37** CHAPTER FIVE
## Other Storms

**44** GLOSSARY
**45** SELECTED BIBLIOGRAPHY
**46** FURTHER READING
**46** WEBSITES
**47** INDEX

## | INTRODUCTION |

L ightning flashes across the sky. Thunder crashes
and rumbles. The lights blink out. From the dark,
you watch the awesome fury of the storm.

Storms are the most dramatic weather events.
Tornadoes destroy lives and property. Hurricanes can
kill thousands. They cause billions of dollars worth of
damage. Where does all that destructive force come
from?

Sunlight provides the energy for all weather—
including storms. Sunlight warms Earth's surface.

It causes water on the ocean's surface to evaporate, or change from liquid to gas. A storm's energy comes from the sun's heat. Understanding storms involves four Cs: convection, condensation, convergence, and the Coriolis effect.

As the sun heats Earth, the surface warms the air above. The heated air rises. Meanwhile, cool air sinks and replaces the rising warm air. That continual movement of warm and cool air is called convection.

*Condensation* means "changing from gas to liquid." Air contains water vapor. Water vapor is a gas. When the vapor condenses, it changes into droplets of liquid water. Condensation also releases energy. The water droplets form clouds and rain, and the energy warms the surrounding air. That warm air then rises higher, and more water vapor condenses. Storm clouds build up into the sky in this way.

# DEMONSTRATING CONVECTION

You can see convection for yourself in a large cooking pot full of tap water. You'll need a small bottle of food coloring with a dropper. *Don't try this without an adult around.*

Put the bottle of food coloring in the refrigerator to cool. Fill the cooking pot with water. Place it on the stove. Let it sit untouched for at least half an hour. This lets the water become still and reach room temperature.

Take the food coloring out of the refrigerator. Gently drop several drops of food coloring into the water. Most of the cold dye will sink to the bottom, as cool air does. With an adult's help, turn the stove burner on low. Soon you'll see the dye start to rise as it warms.

Air pressure is the weight of the air pressing down on Earth. Warm, rising air has low pressure. Cool, sinking air has high pressure. Winds always blow from areas of high pressure to areas of low pressure.

All around a low-pressure area, winds flow inward toward the center of low pressure. This is called convergence. The converging winds push more air upward. The rising air cools. Its water vapor condenses, creating storm clouds. The low-pressure storm system is called a cyclone.

Cyclones spin as winds blow. They spin because Earth spins in space. Earth's spinning motion bends the paths of objects moving across the surface. This is called the Coriolis effect. It bends converging winds. They spiral toward the center of a cyclone. Cyclones spin counterclockwise north of

Converging Winds North of the Equator

low-pressure center

winds bent to the right

counter-clockwise rotation

WINDS BLOW TOWARD A CENTER OF LOW PRESSURE. NORTH OF THE EQUATOR, THEY BEND TO THE RIGHT. THIS MAKES THE LOW-PRESSURE CENTER SPIN COUNTERCLOCKWISE.

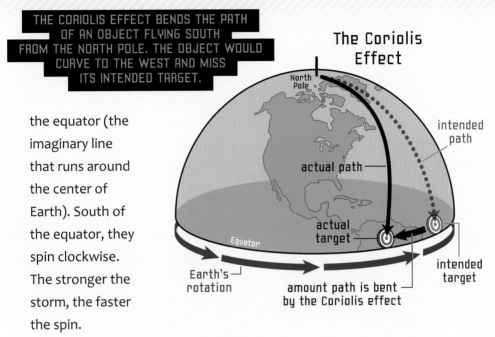

THE CORIOLIS EFFECT BENDS THE PATH OF AN OBJECT FLYING SOUTH FROM THE NORTH POLE. THE OBJECT WOULD CURVE TO THE WEST AND MISS ITS INTENDED TARGET.

## The Coriolis Effect

North Pole

intended path

actual path

actual target

Equator

Earth's rotation

amount path is bent by the Coriolis effect

intended target

the equator (the imaginary line that runs around the center of Earth). South of the equator, they spin clockwise. The stronger the storm, the faster the spin.

These four processes help create the storms that blow across Earth. Convection sets the air in motion. Condensation creates clouds and rain. Convergence brings more moisture and wind to the center of a storm system. And the Coriolis effect gives storms their spin.

| CHAPTER ONE |

# AIR MASSES, WEATHER FRONTS, AND MIDLATITUDE CYCLONES

Air that stays over the desert for several days becomes hot and dry. Air above the balmy Gulf of Mexico gets warm and humid (wet). In winter, air above chilly northern Canada gets very cold.

These large regions of air are called air masses. An air mass has two important traits—temperature and humidity (the amount of water vapor in the air). Together, they give an air mass its density. Cold, dry air is dense. That means its molecules, or tiniest particles, are packed more tightly. Warm, humid air is less dense.

Air masses don't stay in one place. Global wind patterns move them from one part of the world to another. As they move, air masses bump into one another. Storms often form when warm, humid air meets cold, dry air.

## WEATHER FRONTS

The boundary between two air masses is called a front. A weather front is not a sharp line. It is a zone—a wide area where the two air masses meet.

Weather fronts often create rain and storms. Cold air is denser and heavier than warm air. When air masses meet, cold air stays near Earth's surface. The warmer air rises above the cold air. As the warm air rises, it gets cooler. Water vapor condenses and clouds form. Clouds can bring rain.

Sometimes a cold air mass moves in to replace a warm air mass. The leading edge of the cold air mass is called a cold front. The cold air pushes under the warmer air. The warm air rises quickly.

Storms along a cold front often bring strong winds, thunder, and lightning. But they usually do not last long. Cold fronts are not very

## Cold Front

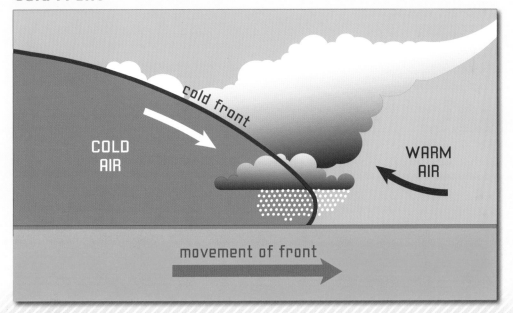

wide, and they move quickly. A cold front usually passes in just a few hours. As a cold front passes, the temperature drops. The air feels drier. The wind usually changes direction. The sky clears quickly.

On a weather map, a cold front is marked by a blue line. Blue triangles point in the direction the front is moving.

Sometimes a warm air mass moves in to replace a cold air mass. A warm front forms where the edge of the warm air mass meets the colder air. The warm air gradually pushes over the cold air.

A warm front covers a wide area. Clouds in a warm front can form a band more than 500 miles (800 kilometers) wide. Rains from a warm front are gentler and last longer than rains from a cold front. Warm fronts also move more slowly than cold fronts.

On a weather map, a red line stands for a warm front. Red half circles point in the direction the front is moving.

## Warm Front

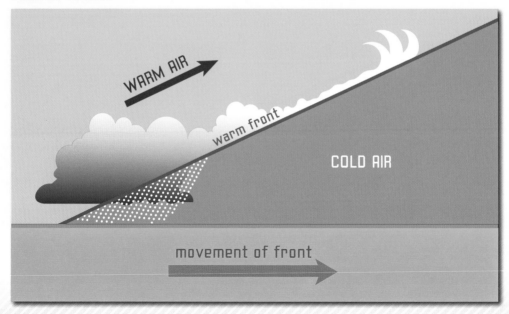

WARM AIR

warm front

COLD AIR

movement of front

Sometimes two air masses sit side by side. Neither air mass can push the other out of the way. This is a stationary front. *Stationary* means "standing still." If one of the air masses has a lot of moisture, the weather will be rainy or cloudy.

On a weather map, a stationary front is marked by a line of alternating red and blue shapes. Red half circles point in one direction. Blue triangles point in the other. The red and blue shapes show which directions the air masses were moving before they met.

A fourth type of front is an occluded front. Occluded fronts form when a fast-moving cold front catches up to a slower-moving warm front. An occluded front squeezes warm air up above two colder air masses—the cold air that was ahead of the warm front and the cold air that caught up to the warm front. Occluded fronts may act like warm fronts or cold fronts. It depends on which cool air mass is colder.

## Occluded Fronts

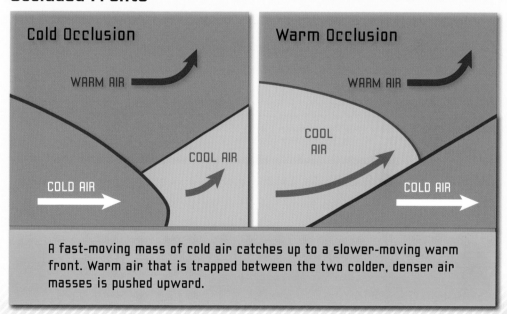

A fast-moving mass of cold air catches up to a slower-moving warm front. Warm air that is trapped between the two colder, denser air masses is pushed upward.

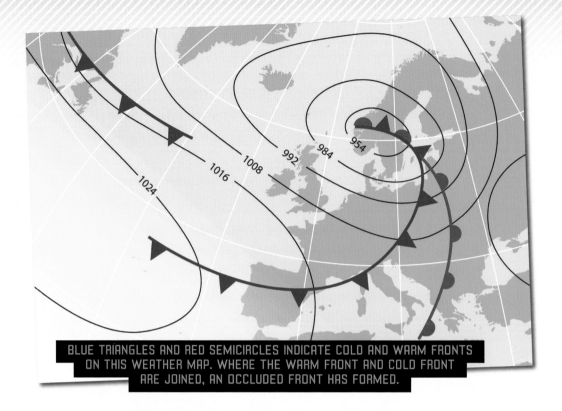

BLUE TRIANGLES AND RED SEMICIRCLES INDICATE COLD AND WARM FRONTS ON THIS WEATHER MAP. WHERE THE WARM FRONT AND COLD FRONT ARE JOINED, AN OCCLUDED FRONT HAS FORMED.

Television forecasters may just call occluded fronts cold fronts or warm fronts, since they act in similar ways.

On a weather map, a purple line or a line of alternating red and blue stands for an occluded front. Triangles and half circles point in the direction of the overtaking front.

## MIDLATITUDE CYCLONES

In North America, storms often form when air masses collide. Frigid air sweeps south behind a cold front from Canada. The cold air moves alongside warm, humid air from the Gulf of Mexico heading north behind a warm front. A front forms where the edges of the air masses meet.

The movement of the air masses in different directions creates wind shear. Wind shear is a change in wind speed or direction over a short distance. An area of low pressure forms along the front as warm air rises over the cold air. Due to the Coriolis effect, the wind begins to spin counterclockwise around the center of this low pressure. The storm strengthens as the warm, moist air converges toward the storm center. The air pressure drops even more. The wind spirals over a huge area. A midlatitude cyclone is born.

Midlatitude cyclones are areas of low pressure that form between 30 and 60 degrees latitude (the middle latitudes). The storm grows until the fast-moving cold front overtakes the slower-moving warm front. An occluded front forms. As the warm air is lifted above the ground, the storm loses its energy. It then gradually weakens.

# WHY DO CYCLONIC WINDS SPIN?

Try this: Put a pencil between the palms of your hands. Hold the pencil so it points up. The pencil represents the low pressure center of a storm.

Imagine your right hand is the warm air mass that is moving north. Your left hand is the cold air mass moving south. Slowly slide your right hand away from you. Slide your left hand toward you at the same time. What happens to the pencil? It spins counterclockwise.

# CYCLONES

The word *cyclone* can be confusing. It is used for several different kinds of storms. Some people use it to mean tornado. Hurricanes in the Indian Ocean are also called cyclones. But to scientists, a cyclone is the wind circling any low-pressure system.

Midlatitude cyclones are the most common large storms in the United States. These cyclones are huge. They can cover many thousands of square miles. Viewed from space, their clouds form the shape of a huge comma.

Forecasters may simply call these cyclones low-pressure systems, or storms. Along the Atlantic coast of the United States, midlatitude cyclones are called nor'easters. That's because their movement and strongest winds come from the northeast.

Midlatitude cyclones can be very destructive. They bring heavy rain, snow, and wind. They may cause flooding, power outages, traffic delays, and even deaths.

THIS MIDLATITUDE CYCLONE BROUGHT UP TO 24 INCHES (60 CENTIMETERS) OF SNOW TO NORTH DAKOTA, SOUTH DAKOTA, MONTANA, AND WYOMING IN APRIL 2006.

## CHAPTER TWO

# THUNDERSTORMS

It's a warm summer afternoon. The sun is high overhead. As the sun's energy heats the land, water evaporates from Earth. Warm air rises upward in large bubbles called thermals.

Water vapor carries energy into the atmosphere (a blanket of air surrounding Earth). As the air rises, it cools. Water vapor condenses. This process forms cumulus clouds—puffy white clouds with distinct edges and flat bases. The condensation also releases energy. This rewarms the air. The air rises higher. The clouds grow larger and larger.

An anvil-shaped cumulonimbus cloud stretches high into the air. This type of cloud can mean thunder and lightning are likely.

Outside the cloud, cooler, drier air flows downward. It replaces the warm air rising into the cloud. The up-and-down air currents are called convection currents. Swirling winds surge inside the cloud.

If the air is warm and humid enough, the cloud soon reaches miles into the air. Its top spreads out. It forms the flattened shape of an anvil. The bottom of the cloud is dark. It has become a cumulonimbus cloud—a thunderhead.

In the upper regions of the cloud, ice pellets freeze. They fall through the cloud. Tiny droplets of water freeze to the pellets. The ice gets heavier. As it falls through warmer air below, it melts and turns to rain. If the pellets grow large enough, they fall as hail.

All the movement within the cloud builds up a type of electricity. The electrical charge gets stronger and stronger. Finally, lightning flashes, releasing the charge. The heat of the lightning causes sound waves, which we hear as thunder.

As rain falls, it cools the cloud. The falling raindrops pull cool air down with them in currents called downdrafts. The rain and downdrafts cool the air below the cloud. This cooling takes away the storm's energy. Without warm air below, the storm weakens. After a half hour or so, all that's left is a few clouds.

Air mass thunderstorms are storms that develop within an air mass this way. Air mass thunderstorms form on warm, humid days. They are usually small. They don't last long. The United States has about one hundred thousand thunderstorms each year.

About 10 percent of these thunderstorms are considered severe. A severe thunderstorm has winds over 58 miles (93 km) per hour or hailstones at least 0.75 inches (1.9 cm) wide, or both.

Severe thunderstorms usually form ahead of a cold front. This happens most often in spring and early summer. The denser cold air pushes warm air upward. Clouds form in a line of towering thunderheads. The line of storms is called a squall line.

THE LEFT EDGE OF THIS CLOUD BANK SHOWS THE FRONT OF A SQUALL LINE. HEAVY RAIN SHOWERS FOLLOW.

Severe thunderstorms act differently from ordinary thunderstorms. Downdrafts of cold air create powerful microbursts of wind—especially strong downdrafts over a small area. Wind shear tilts the downdrafts ahead of the storm. They don't rob the storm of energy. Instead, they keep pushing more warm air up into the storm. This type of thunderstorm can last for hours. It may travel for hundreds of miles.

About three thousand severe storms in the United States each year are powerful supercell storms. In these huge thunderstorms, wind shear causes the upward current to rotate within the storm cloud. Forecasters watch supercells closely. They are the most likely storms to produce tornadoes.

SCIENTISTS KNOW THAT THIS TYPE OF SUPERCELL CLOUD COULD PRODUCE TORNADOES.

## LIGHTNING AND THUNDER

Rub your socks along a carpet on a dry day. Then touch a doorknob. Did you feel a little spark? You just made lightning! Lightning is an electric spark—a big one. It's powerful enough to jump from a cloud to the ground or from cloud to cloud.

A spark jumps when the electrical charge between two places is unbalanced. During a thunderstorm, the upper part of a cloud becomes positively charged. The lower part is negatively charged. The storm also creates a positive charge on the ground below. When the charges are strong enough, lightning flashes between them. The lightning evens out the imbalance.

Air is not a good conductor, or carrier, of electricity. So the imbalance must be very high before a spark can jump. A lightning bolt has a force of more than 3 million volts per meter. In comparison, the electricity running to outlets in U.S. homes is just 120 volts.

# A Flash of Lightning

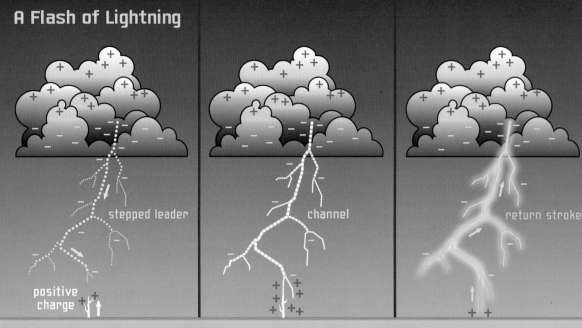

| | | |
|---|---|---|
| stepped leader | channel | return stroke |
| positive charge | | |

A stepped leader flows down from the cloud. A positive charge shoots up from the ground.

The positive charge meets the stepped leader, forming a channel from the ground to the cloud.

Powerful electricity flows back up the channel. This return stroke makes a bright flash.

Lightning bolts seem to strike in an instant. But they actually move in steps. First, a negative charge flows out from a cloud. It travels about 150 to 300 feet (50 to 100 meters) at a time. After a tiny pause (about 50 millionths of a second), it moves another 150 to 300 feet. This flow is called a stepped leader. It's very faint and moves too quickly for you to see it. But photographers can capture stepped leaders with high-speed cameras.

A positive charge moves up from the ground to meet the stepped leader. This forms a channel through the air.

Electricity then flows through the channel to the ground. Finally, a positively charged return stroke moves back up the channel to the cloud. This stroke makes a bright flash of lightning—the spark you can see. Several strokes often follow one another through the channel. The whole process takes less than a second.

Sometimes the charges are reversed. The bottom of the cloud may be positively charged. The return stroke is negatively charged. This kind of lightning is more common in severe storms than in ordinary thunderstorms.

Lightning creates tremendous heat. The temperature of the air in the lightning channel may reach 54,000°F (30,000°C)! The hot air expands very quickly. It acts like an explosion. Like any explosion, it creates sound waves.

# THUNDERSTORM SAFETY

Many people survive being struck by lightning. But lightning kills almost one hundred people each year in the United States. During a thunderstorm, the safest place is inside a building. Most buildings conduct electricity down into the ground through water pipes and electrical wires in the walls.

Since pipes, wires, and other metals conduct electricity, don't take a shower or do dishes. Don't use a landline telephone. (Cell phones are okay.) Stay away from doors and windows with metal frames.

Outside, the safest place is in a car. Lightning flows around the outside of the car's metal frame, but not the inside. If you're not near a car, avoid tall objects and high ground. Lightning often strikes the tallest object in an area. Stay away from metal objects and water. Don't stand under a lone tree or shelter. Find a low piece of ground. Crouch down to keep your body low. But don't lie flat—electricity from a lightning strike can flow across the ground.

Most important, don't wait until the storm gets close! If you see lightning or hear thunder, go inside right away.

# TIMING A LIGHTNING STRIKE

We see lightning before we hear the thunder. That's because light travels much faster than sound. Light travels 186,000 miles (300,000 km) per second. We see the flash almost instantly. Sound moves through air at about 0.2 miles (0.3 km) per second. So the sound arrives at our ears much later.

Here's how to estimate how far away a lightning strike was. Start counting seconds when you see the flash. Stop when you hear the thunder. Sound travels about 1 mile (1.6 km) in five seconds. If you counted to ten, the strike was about 2 miles (3.2 km) away. If you counted to fifteen, it was 3 miles (about 5 km) away.

Sound moves outward from the lightning strike. Nearby, you hear a loud crack and boom of thunder. The farther the sound spreads, the weaker it becomes. Distant thunder sounds like a gentle rumble. It lasts longer because the sound echoes off other objects. Thunder startles people. But it's the lightning that's dangerous. It can start fires and damage trees and buildings. A lightning strike can also injure or kill people.

## CHAPTER THREE

# TORNADOES

A spinning column of air snakes down from a dark, churning cloud. The funnel cloud reaches the ground. It has become a tornado. It blasts everything in its path. Some tornadoes travel for 200 miles (322 km) or more. Winds inside can reach 300 miles (483 km) per hour. These funnel clouds can be more than 1 mile (1.6 km) wide.

Most tornadoes are not that big. The average tornado is 300 to 2,000 feet (91 to 610 m) wide.

Many are smaller. On average, tornadoes stay on the ground for about 4 miles (6 km). They travel about 30 miles (48 km) per hour. The average tornado has winds of 100 miles (161 km) per hour or less.

Tornadoes are most common in spring and early summer. That's when cold fronts collide with warm, humid air. Severe thunderstorms and supercells form. Tornadoes most often form in supercells.

Scientists think tornadoes begin as wind shear. Winds at different levels of the atmosphere blow in different directions. This creates a spinning effect. A sideways column of air begins rotating beneath or within a cumulonimbus cloud.

A strong updraft then tilts up the rotating air into the thundercloud. A spinning column of air forms inside the storm. Warm, moist air converges at the storm's lower level. This air adds more energy and strengthens the twisting motion.

A tornado ripped through this home in Parkersburg, Iowa, in 2008.

The column of spinning air narrows. It rotates faster. A whirling tube of air—a tornado—drops from the base of the cloud. You can't always see this spiral of air.

Air pressure inside the tornado is very low. Air rushes toward the tornado. Moisture condenses in the spiral, forming a funnel cloud. The funnel cloud makes the tornado easier to see. When the spiral touches down, it picks up dust and larger objects. Then the tornado becomes darker and more visible.

## FORECASTING TORNADOES

Tornadoes are very hard to predict. No one knows if or when a tornado will touch down. Forecasters only know when one might form. And it's impossible to know how strong it may be. Even measuring and studying tornadoes is difficult. Scientists need to have weather instruments in exactly the right place at the right time.

# TORNADO ALLEY

The United States has about one thousand tornadoes each year. That's more than any other country. Tornadoes occur in all fifty states. But they are much more common in some places than others.

Tornado Alley gets the most by far. It's a region in the central United States, including Oklahoma and parts of Kansas, Nebraska, and Texas. Other nearby states also get more tornadoes than other parts of the country. Cold air from Canada meets warm air from the Gulf of Mexico in this area. The colliding air masses can create a lot of violent weather.

A TORNADO RIPS ACROSS NEBRASKA. IT APPEARS LIGHT IN COLOR BECAUSE SUNLIGHT IS STRIKING THE SIDE WE SEE.

However, better weather technology has improved tornado safety. The average number of U.S. tornado deaths each year has dropped in the past fifty years. In the United States, tornadoes kill an average of about sixty people a year. This is mostly because of better warnings. Doppler radar uses radio waves to measure the direction and speed of moisture moving through the air. It often lets forecasters see tornadoes forming before they touch down.

# THE FUJITA SCALE

In the 1960s, meteorologist T. Theodore Fujita *(right)* created a way to measure the strength of tornadoes. The scale is based on the damage a storm causes. Scientists updated the scale in 2007 based on newer information about wind speed and damage. The new version is called the Enhanced Fujita (EF) Scale.

| Scale | Wind Speed in miles (km) per hour | Damage Examples |
|-------|-----------------------------------|-----------------|
| EF0 | 65–85 (105–137) | Light: tree branches broken; siding, shingles and billboards damaged |
| EF1 | 86–110 (138–177) | Moderate: trees snapped, windows broken, mobile homes pushed off foundations |
| EF2 | 111–135 (178–217) | Considerable: large trees uprooted, roofs torn off frame buildings, mobile homes destroyed |
| EF3 | 136–165 (218–266) | Severe: trees leveled, cars overturned, walls removed from buildings |
| EF4 | 166–200 (266–322) | Devastating: well-constructed houses destroyed, cars and other heavy objects thrown through the air |
| EF5 | over 200 (322) | Incredible: structures the size of autos thrown more than 109 yards (100 m), steel-reinforced structures highly damaged, bark removed from trees |

A DOPPLER RADAR IMAGE SHOWS SEVERE THUNDERSTORM ACTIVITY OVER TEXAS AND OKLAHOMA, INCLUDING AREAS WHERE TORNADOES WOULD LIKELY FORM.

The National Weather Service is the U.S. organization responsible for forecasting the weather. It issues a tornado watch if there is a possibility of tornadoes. This group issues a tornado warning when one is spotted on radar or by a person. A tornado watch tells you to be prepared. A tornado warning means you should take cover right away.

The safest place to go is an underground shelter or basement. If that's not possible, move to the center of a sturdy building. Stay on the lowest floor. A small room like a bathroom or closet is best. Stay away from windows. If you're stuck outside, lie flat in a ditch or other low ground. Cover your head.

## FASCINATING FACT:

Flash floods (floods that rise and fall quickly) kill more people than any other weather event. Lightning is second, and tornadoes are third.

## CHAPTER FOUR
# HURRICANES

No storm is more destructive than a hurricane. This type of cyclone has winds swirling at 74 miles (119 km) per hour or faster. Hurricanes develop over the ocean, usually between 10 degrees and 20 degrees latitude—not far from the equator in the Mid-Atlantic, Eastern Pacific, or Indian oceans. East winds (winds from the east) usually push the storms toward the west. Hurricane season happens during summer and fall. Ocean water is warmest then.

# Where Tropical Cyclones Strike

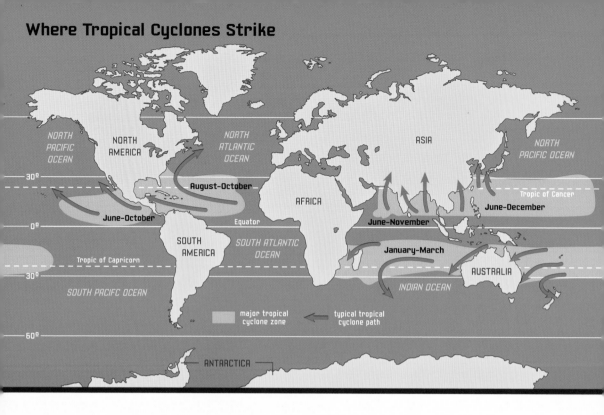

Hurricanes strike in several parts of the world. They are called different things in different places. Hurricanes in Southeast Asia are called cyclones. In the western Pacific, they are called typhoons. The word hurricane is used in the eastern Pacific and the Atlantic Ocean. But these are all the same type of storm. Scientists call them tropical cyclones.

A hurricane begins as an area of low air pressure over warm ocean water. Humid air converges toward the low pressure. As the air rises, water vapor condenses into clouds.

When the vapor condenses, its energy is released. The air warms and rises higher. Thunderstorms develop. Meteorologists (scientists who study the weather) call the cluster of storms a tropical disturbance.

The thunderclouds build. More warm, humid air moves in to replace the rising air. This fuels more clouds and storms. The wind begins to circle around the low-pressure center, due to the Coriolis effect.

This stage of the storm is called a tropical depression. A tropical depression has winds from 23 to 38 miles (37 to 61 km) per hour.

If conditions are right, the storm continues to grow. The winds spiral faster. Clouds and rainbands (bands of storm clouds) spiral inward. Humid air feeds more energy into the storm. When the winds are between 40 and 73 miles (65 and 117 km) per hour, the storm is considered a tropical storm.

Think of the growing storm as a spinning heat engine. Warm, humid air enters the storm at its lower level. This air converges toward the center of the storm and rises around it. The water vapor condenses. It releases its heat, causing the air to rise even more. Air at the top of the storm spreads out. This makes room for more warm, humid air to enter below.

A tropical storm forms above the Gulf of Mexico. The swirling clouds create a spiral.

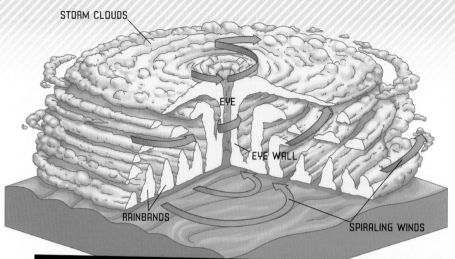

STORM CLOUDS

EYE

EYE WALL

RAINBANDS

SPIRALING WINDS

WIND AND RAINBANDS SPIRAL AROUND A HURRICANE'S CALM EYE. THE EYE IS OFTEN 20 TO 40 MILES (32 TO 64 KM) WIDE, WHILE THE WHOLE STORM OFTEN REACHES ABOUT 300 MILES (483 KM) ACROSS.

When the wind reaches 74 miles (119 km) per hour, the storm is a hurricane. A small region of fair weather and light winds forms at the storm center. This is the storm's eye. Heavy clouds surround the eye. This is the eye wall. That's where the wind and rain are heaviest.

Most hurricanes last a week or less. Hurricanes remain strong while they spin over warm ocean water. They weaken when they move over land. The land robs them of energy and slows the wind.

Strong upper-level winds can also weaken a hurricane. They blow away the tops of the clouds and interrupt the heat engine. A cold front may turn the storm northward, over cooler water. This also takes away the storm's energy.

Once a hurricane hits land, it can do terrible damage before losing its energy. Hurricane winds can reach 150 miles (241 km) per hour or more. The wind can uproot trees, tear buildings apart, and throw large pieces of debris through the air. It may produce tornadoes. Over the ocean, the wind also pushes up huge water waves—sometimes 30 feet (10 m) high or more.

# THE SAFFIR-SIMPSON HURRICANE WIND SCALE

Meteorologists compare the strength of hurricanes on a scale from 1 to 5. Herbert Saffir and Bob Simpson introduced the scale in 1971. The National Weather Service uses a revised version of the scale, based on peak wind speed.

| Category | Wind Speed in miles (km) per hour | Damage Examples |
|---|---|---|
| 1 | 74–95 (119–153) | Damaging winds. Some damage to buildings, mainly to unanchored mobile homes |
| 2 | 96–110 (154–177) | Very strong winds with widespread damage. Some roofing, door, and window damage. Considerable damage to mobile homes likely |
| 3 | 111–130 (178–209) | Dangerous winds with extensive damage. Some structural damage to houses and buildings with a minor amount of wall failures (cracking or collapsing). Older mobile homes are destroyed. |
| 4 | 131–155 (210–249) | Extremely dangerous winds with devastating damage. Some wall failures and complete roof failures (caving in) on houses. All signs are blown down. Complete destruction of mobile homes |
| 5 | >155 (249) | Catastrophic damage. Complete roof failure on many homes and industrial buildings. Some complete building failures, with small buildings blown over or away |

A hurricane can also drop 25 inches (64 cm) of rain in a day. This often causes flooding. The rain damages buildings that have lost roofs or windows.

The worst damage comes from storm surge. Storm surge is ocean water pushed toward the shore, ahead of the storm, by strong winds. The surge is more than just high waves. Storm surge can add 20 feet (6 m) to normal water levels.

New Orleans, Louisiana, and the nearby Gulf coast experienced all that when Hurricane Katrina hit on August 29, 2005. More than eighteen hundred people died in the storm damage and flooding. Hundreds of thousands became homeless. Katrina destroyed more than $80 billion worth of property.

# NAMING HURRICANES

A storm is named once its winds reach tropical storm strength, 40 miles (64 km) per hour. Meteorologists began giving women's names to tropical storms around 1940. In 1978 the U.S. National Hurricane Center began alternating male and female names. The storms are named alphabetically, starting with A. (The list leaves out Q, U, and Z.) So many storms took place in 2005 that the entire list was used. The last few storms of that season were named with Greek letters.

The Hurricane Center uses six lists of names. After six years, names are reused. But when a storm causes major damage, its name is retired. So the name Katrina won't be used again.

Many people took shelter in tents after Cyclone Nargis hit Myanmar in 2008. The hurricane left millions homeless.

In Southeast Asia, tropical cyclones are often more deadly. Many people live in low-lying areas that flood easily. Limited roads and transportation make it hard for people to leave quickly. In 1970 a tropical cyclone killed more than 300,000 people in Bangladesh. And in 2008, Cyclone Nargis killed at least 140,000 people when it struck Myanmar (Burma).

The winds that guide a hurricane's path are often unpredictable. Before weather satellites and radar could track them, hurricanes often struck with little warning. Modern technology lets forecasters see these storms days in advance.

CYCLONE NARGIS HOVERS IN THE BAY OF BENGAL BEFORE STRIKING THE MYANMAR COAST.

A METEOROLOGIST AT THE NATIONAL HURRICANE CENTER IN MIAMI, FLORIDA, TRACKS A HURRICANE USING COMPUTERS AND SATELLITE IMAGERY.

Forecasters declare a hurricane watch long before most hurricanes threaten land. As the storm moves closer, they announce a hurricane warning where the storm is most likely to hit. The early warnings help. People can evacuate (leave) the area ahead of time or prepare to stay safe indoors. Over the past thirty years, the average number of hurricane deaths in the United States has been about fifty per year. (The year of Katrina and Rita, 2005, was much deadlier than average.)

Recently, scientists have learned that hurricanes expand and contract as they move. When a storm contracts, it gets smaller. But its winds blow faster. It's like a spinning skater who pulls his or her arms close to the body. The skater's spinning speed increases. As a hurricane expands, the winds slow. Expanding or contracting can quickly change the strength of a storm before it hits land.

## CHAPTER FIVE
# OTHER STORMS

Thunderstorms, tornadoes, and hurricanes capture our attention. They are powerful. They can be frightening. But weather brings other kinds of storms too.

During the spring or fall, we might have gentle rainstorms. In the winter, we might get snow or sleet. Depending on climate, the ever-changing weather may bring several other kinds of storms our way.

## BLIZZARDS

Snow falls when moisture in clouds freezes into tiny ice crystals. More and more water freezes onto the crystals until they are heavy enough to fall. If they remain frozen as they fall through cold air, they fall as snowflakes. A winter snowstorm can be beautiful. It blankets the ground in white. But a blizzard is a dangerous storm.

A MAN BRAVES BLIZZARD WINDS TO SHOVEL SNOW FROM A SIDEWALK IN NEW YORK CITY.

How is a blizzard different from an ordinary snowstorm? A blizzard has strong winds along with cold and snow. A blizzard has winds greater than 35 miles (56 km) per hour. The storm lasts for at least three hours. The temperature is 20°F (–7°C) or lower. And in a blizzard, you can see less than 0.25 miles (0.4 km) ahead. There is too much blowing snow to see farther.

The wind blows the falling snow. It also lifts the snow that has already fallen and piles it into tall snowdrifts. The air is full of snowflakes. The snow makes driving difficult and slippery.

Even walking outside can be dangerous. The wind makes the air feel colder. The wind takes heat from your body as it blows across your skin. So your body can become dangerously cold very fast if you are outside during a blizzard.

A severe blizzard is especially threatening. Winds in a severe blizzard blow at more than 45 miles (72 km) per hour, and the temperature is 10°F (–12°C) or lower. Seeing just a short distance ahead is hard.

Blizzards often form in midlatitude cyclones. These snowy storms usually don't do much damage. But if a storm system is large enough, a blizzard can last for days. People may have to wait out the storm at home.

## ICE STORMS

An ice storm is another dangerous cold-weather storm. It is also called freezing rain. In an ice storm, cold raindrops fall through freezing air. They become cooler than the freezing point (32°F, or 0°C). As soon as they touch the ground, they freeze and form glaze. Everything gets coated with this glaze of ice.

Ice storms are often worse than heavy snow. The ice weighs down trees and power lines. Branches and wires snap. Electricity and telephone service can be cut off. Icy roads are unsafe for driving. It can take weeks for an area to recover and make repairs after a big ice storm.

After an ice storm, tree branches are coated in a layer of ice.

## DUST STORMS AND SANDSTORMS

Over dry regions, wind may pick up huge amounts of dust from the ground. Clouds of dust darken the sky. Dust whips through the air. If winds are strong—more than 30 miles (48 km) per hour—and the blowing dust makes it hard to see far, the storm is called a dust storm. The choking dust makes it almost impossible for people to stay outside. Tiny dust particles damage machinery. The dust sifts into buildings through window and door frames.

The traveling dust particles affect the weather after the storm too. The dust remains in the atmosphere. Water vapor condenses on bits of dust. The condensation forms clouds and rain. So a dust storm somewhere in the world could cause rain thousands of miles away.

Sandstorms can form when the wind blows over sandy areas. They sometimes grow to great size. In 2001 a huge sandstorm blew across the Sahara, a desert in Africa. It covered an area larger than the state of California.

A sandstorm sweeps across the sky in western Africa.

# DROUGHT

A drought is a long period with little or no rain. Droughts are harmful weather events. People need water to drink. We need it to grow crops.

In the 1930s, the Great Plains in the United States had a drought that lasted for years. Crops would not grow. The soil dried out. Without crops covering the land, many tons of topsoil blew away during the Dust Bowl years. Many people moved to other parts of the country.

Earth's surface has been getting slightly warmer in recent years. As Earth's climate changes, drought may become worse in some areas. Meanwhile, other regions may get more rainfall.

People can't prevent drought, but they can reduce its effects. They can water crops using more efficient methods or grow crops that need less water. They can also plant trees and other plants to hold moisture in the soil and slow the wind.

The United States also has sandstorms and dust storms. During the 1930s, the central United States suffered a severe drought (lack of rain). Dust storms swept across the plains.

## DUST DEVILS

Dust devils are whirlwinds—small, rotating windstorms. They form in hot, dry regions. The sun's energy heats the land and the air just above it. The air rises and forms a spinning column. The swirling air lifts dust particles, forming a dust devil.

A DUST DEVIL REACHES TOWARD THE SKY IN SOUTH AMERICA'S ATACAMA DESERT, THE DRIEST DESERT ON EARTH.

Dust devils may look like tornadoes. But they are very different. Tornadoes form in thunderstorms. They descend from the clouds. Dust devils form on the ground. They spiral up into the air. Their wind speed may reach 85 miles (136 km) per hour. That's strong enough to do damage. However, most are much weaker, with winds of only 5 to 15 miles (8 to 24 km) per hour. And dust devils don't last long before they die away.

## WATERSPOUTS

A waterspout is a whirlwind that forms over water. Some waterspouts descend from thunderstorms, like tornadoes. These storms can be quite damaging.

However, most waterspouts form beneath fair weather cumulus clouds. Fair weather waterspouts are more like dust devils. Their wind is weaker than a tornado's—usually less than 50 miles (80 km) per hour. A waterspout does not suck water into its funnel cloud. But it kicks up plenty of spray as it moves across the water.

People in southern Florida see waterspouts quite often. Fair weather waterspouts may look like tornadoes. But they are smaller and less dangerous. Most waterspouts last no more than ten to fifteen minutes.

## VIOLENT, HELPFUL WEATHER

A WATERSPOUT TOUCHES DOWN OFF THE COAST OF GREECE.

Storms can cause great damage. They even take lives. But they also bring life-giving rain and snow. A thunderstorm can end a drought. A hurricane can fill lakes and reservoirs with water. A blanket of snow protects plants and animals from harsh winter temperatures. Mountain snow from winter storms melts slowly, keeping rivers flowing during the summer months. Storms are a necessary part of the world's weather.

# GLOSSARY

**air mass:** a large body of air with similar temperature and humidity throughout

**air mass thunderstorms:** also called thundershowers; thunderstorms that form within a mass of warm, humid air

**air pressure:** the force of air pushing down on Earth. High air pressure usually brings fair weather, and low pressure brings storms.

**blizzard:** a severe snowstorm with winds greater than 35 miles (56 km) per hour and temperatures of 20°F (–7°C) or lower

**cold front:** the leading edge of a cold air mass moving in to replace warm air. Cold air pushes under the warm air at the cold front.

**condensation:** the process of changing from a gas to a liquid

**convection:** vertical (up or down) movement in a gas or liquid caused by temperature differences

**convergence:** the movement of air toward the center of a low-pressure system

**Coriolis effect:** a bending of the path of any object moving over Earth's surface. Earth's rotation in space causes the Coriolis effect.

**cumulonimbus cloud:** a very tall thunderstorm cloud

**cyclone:** a region of low pressure with winds that circle counterclockwise in the Northern Hemisphere. Cyclones usually produce storms.

**dust devil:** a small, spinning wind that becomes visible as it picks up dust and dirt from Earth's surface

**eye:** a region with calm winds and clear skies at the center of a hurricane

**front:** the zone where two different air masses meet

**glaze:** a thin coating of ice that forms when freezing rain falls on a cold surface

**hurricane:** a huge, spinning storm with heavy rain and powerful winds that forms in areas near the equator. Hurricanes are called typhoons or cyclones in Asia, but the scientific term for all these storms is tropical cyclone.

**ice storm:** freezing rain; a storm with very cold rain that freezes and turns to a glaze of ice as soon as it hits Earth's surface

**lightning:** a powerful electric spark produced by a thunderstorm

**microburst:** a powerful downdraft of wind beneath a thunderstorm

**midlatitude cyclone:** a large, spinning storm that forms around a center of low pressure between about 30 degrees and 60 degrees latitude

**occluded front:** the boundary between air masses that forms when a fast-moving cold front catches up to a warm front. Occluded fronts may act like warm fronts or cold fronts.

**squall line:** a line of thunderstorms that forms at the leading edge of a cold front

**stationary front:** a boundary between a cold air mass and a warm air mass, with neither able to move and push the other out of the way

**stepped leader:** a flow of electricity that travels in short steps in the first stage of a lightning strike

**storm surge:** a rise in sea level caused by a hurricane's wind pushing ocean water toward the shore

**supercell:** a huge, long-lasting, severe thunderstorm formed within a single storm cloud

**tornado:** a rapidly spinning column of air that extends from the base of a thunderstorm to the ground

**warm front:** the leading edge of a warm air mass moving in to replace colder air. Warm air gradually rises over the cold air at a warm front.

**waterspout:** a spinning column of air that extends from the base of a thunderstorm or cumulus cloud to a body of water

**wind shear:** a large change in wind direction or speed over a short distance

## SELECTED BIBLIOGRAPHY

Aguardo, Edward, and James E. Burt. *Understanding Weather & Climate*. 3rd ed. Upper Saddle River, NJ: Prentice Hall, 2004.

Ahrens, C. Donald. *Meteorology Today*. 8th ed. Belmont, CA: Thompson Higher Education, 2007.

Allaby, Michael. *The Facts on File Weather and Climate Handbook*. New York: Facts on File, 2002.

Lutgens, Frederick, and Edward J. Tarbuck. *The Atmosphere: An Introduction to Meteorology*. 10th ed. Upper Saddle River, NJ: Prentice Hall, 2006.

Nese, Jon M., Leem M. Grenci, David J. Mornhinweg, and Timothy W. Owen. *A World of Weather: Fundamentals of Meteorology*. Dubuque, IA: Kendall/Hunt Publishing Co., 1996.

Sorbjan, Zbigniew. *Hands-On Meteorology*. Boston: American Meteorological Society, 1996.

Wood, Robert W. *Science for Kids: 39 Easy Meteorology Experiments*. Blue Ridge Summit, PA: Tab Books, 1991.

# FURTHER READING

Challoner, Jack. *Hurricane and Tornado*. New York: DK Pub., 2004. This book packs lots of photos and information to help readers learn more about dangerous weather of all kinds.

Fleisher, Paul. *Doppler Radar, Satellites, and Computer Models: The Science of Weather Forecasting*. Minneapolis: Lerner Publications Company, 2011. Get a more in-depth look at the tools and the science that meteorologists use to predict storms and other weather.

Jackson, Donna M. *Extreme Scientists: Exploring Nature's Mysteries from Perilous Places*. Boston: Houghton Mifflin Books for Children, 2009. Follow three scientists who do dangerous work, including one meteorologist who studies hurricanes—by flying into them.

Murphy, Jim. *Blizzard: The Storm That Changed America*. New York: Scholastic Press, 2000. The historic Great Blizzard of 1888, which brought New York City and much of New England to a standstill, is detailed in this book.

Simon, Seymour. *Lightning*. New York: Collins, 2006. Bright photos help this book's simple, clear text explain lightning, including different types, how it occurs, and how it is studied.

Wetterer, Margaret K., and Charles M. Wetterer. *The Snowshoeing Adventure of Milton Daub, Blizzard Trekker*. Minneapolis: Graphic Universe, 2011. This graphic novel tells of the adventures of a twelve-year-old boy who dons homemade snowshoes to bring food and aid his New York City neighbors during the massive blizzard of 1888.

Woods, Michael, and Mary B. Woods. *Hurricanes*. Minneapolis: Lerner Publications Company, 2007. This book takes you inside hurricane disasters, with dramatic images and firsthand survivor stories from some of the worst storms on record. Look for *Tornadoes* and *Blizzards* in the same series, Disasters Up Close.

# WEBSITES

National Severe Storms Laboratory Severe Storms Primer
http://www.nssl.noaa.gov/primer/
Check out this site for more in-depth science about thunderstorms, tornadoes, floods, hail, lightning, and other stormy weather.

Natural Disasters
http://environment.nationalgeographic.com/environment/natural-disasters/
This National Geographic page includes information on many different types of natural disasters, including hurricanes, tornadoes, floods, and lightning storms.

Sky Diary KIDSTORM
http://skydiary.com/kids/
In addition to photos and information about storms, here you'll find several pages about storm chasers. These adventurous people try to get close to storms—often dangerously close—to study them. Follow a typical chase, and learn how you could become a storm chaser someday.

# INDEX

air masses, 8–13, 17, 26

air pressure, 6, 25, 30

atmosphere, 15, 40

blizzard, 37–39

clouds, 5, 15–17, 20, 23–24, 31–32, 42

condensation, 5, 7, 9, 15, 25, 40

convection, 5, 7

convection currents, 16

convergence, 5–7, 13, 24, 31

Coriolis effect, 5, 7, 13, 30

Doppler radar, 26, 28

downdrafts, 17–18

drought, 41

dust storm, 40–41

equator, 6–7

flood, 34–35

hurricanes, 4, 14, 29–37

ice storm, 39

lightning, 4, 19–22, 28

meteorologists, 30

midlatitude cyclones, 12–14, 39

nor'easters, 14

sandstorm, 40–41

squall line, 17

stepped leader, 20

storm surge, 34

sun, 4–5, 15, 41

supercell storms, 18, 24

thunderheads, 16–17

thunderstorm, 17–19, 30, 37, 43

tornadoes, 4, 14, 18, 23–28, 37, 42–43

waterspout, 42–43

water vapor, 5–6, 15, 31, 40

weather front, 9–12; cold front, 9–10, 12,
17, 24, 32; occluded front, 11–13; stationary
front, 11; warm front, 10–13

wind shear, 13, 18, 24

## ABOUT THE AUTHOR

Paul Fleisher is a veteran educator and the author of dozens of science titles for children, including the Secrets of the Universe series, the Early Bird Food Web series, and *The Big Bang* and *Evolution* for the Great Ideas of Science series. He is also the author of *Parasites: Latching On to a Free Lunch*. He lives with his wife in Richmond, Virginia.

## PHOTO ACKNOWLEDGMENTS

The images in this book are used with the permission of: © Flirt/SuperStock, pp. 1, 25; © age fotostock/SuperStock, pp. 3, 38; © SuperStock/SuperStock, p. 4; © Stephen Krasemann/ Stone/Getty Images, p. 6 (top); © Laura Westlund/Independent Picture Service, pp. 6 (bottom), 7, 9, 10, 11, 20, 30; © Steve Vidler/SuperStock, p. 8; © Dorling Kindersley/Getty Images, p. 12; NASA/GSFC, p. 14; © Ed Collacott/Stone/Getty Images, p. 15; © Robert Harding Picture Library/SuperStock, pp. 16, 40, 42, 43; © Ryan McGinnis/Flickr/Getty Images, p. 17; © Philippe Bourseiller/The Image Bank/Getty Images, p. 18; © Thomas Wiewandt/Taxi/Getty Images, p. 19; © Alan R. Moller/Stone/Getty Images, p. 23; © Steve Pope/Getty Images, p. 24; © Jack Novak/SuperStock, p. 26; AP Photo/Jim Bourdier, p. 27; © Gene Blevins/LA Daily News/CORBIS, p. 28; © Stock Connection/SuperStock, p. 29; © StockTrek/SuperStock, p. 31; © Bill Hauser/Independent Picture Service, p. 32; © NOAA via Getty Images, p. 34; © AFP/Getty Images, p. 35 (top); MODIS Rapid Response Team, NASA Goddard Space Flight Center, p. 35 (bottom); © Joe Raedle/Getty Images, p. 36; © Kike Calvo VWPics/SuperStock, p. 37; © Larry W. Smith/Getty Images, p. 39.

Front cover: © Mihai-bogdan Lazar/Dreamstime.com. Back cover: © iStockphoto.com/ Nadezda Firsova.